Thank You!

Thank you to Samantha Jacquest, owner of Blue House Books,
for the excellent editing.

Samantha Jacquest, Owner
BHBKenosha@gmail.com • 262-484-1776
Find Blue House Books On Facebook, Instagram, and Twitter. @BHBKenosha

BLUE**HOUSE**BOOKS

Thank you to Becky at Skyprint for formatting this book.

The Lord will fight for you, you need only to be still

Exodus 14:14

Foreword

My story is one of love and tragedy. It is my daughter's journey through mental illness and her devastating death at the age of 18. She was injected with a lethal dose of drugs by someone else.

When Tehya was 14 and at a stable point in her life, she wrote in her journal about God, bullying, self-harm, and social media. She had hoped to one day share her thoughts with middle school students to help them as they traveled their own paths. She wrote this journal in 2013. Tehya was under the care of a psychiatrist and taking medication for ADHD and anxiety. She was doing well while on this regimen.

I'm sharing her words now because I'm sure she would want people to know her struggles so they wouldn't feel alone. She loved to help others, especially those left out or hurting. The following passages are in her own words.

Chapter 1

He is Here

I had always been skeptical of God. **But tonight,** I don't even know what happened. I felt a wave of happiness. He was with me. I know it. I told myself I was the worst Christian. I always believed in God, but, I felt resentment towards Him. I thought, "What has He done for me?" Well, I thought He didn't care or I didn't matter. Sunday was always dreaded. I felt no connections with ANYONE at church. I felt unwelcome.

Tonight was remarkable! I started crying, I am not even kidding. It wasn't tears of sorrow, but, of realization and joy. He is HERE! He always has been.

I just realized it today. I closed my eyes and let the beauty of faith and the Lord wash over me. I think I have some depression from stress. Every night before I go to bed, I always think about everything I've messed up and how much I disappoint everyone who counts on me to make safe smart decisions. I didn't know where to turn or do. I made the worst decision I could have. I went towards self-harm. I have cut, burned, and bruised myself. I felt I deserved it. I struggled to overcome it. Music helped and is important to me. I used to be suicidal, but, in a song

I listen to, the lyrics say how everyone needs you no matter what. We are a match made in Heaven; a team we are in this together. I cried and didn't talk at school the next day. I used to feel as if I wasn't needed on earth and that I had no purpose for anything. Sure, I could sing and write, but how does that help people? I vowed when I started hurting myself, no one would find out. I focused all my energy on my friends. If they were sad, I would do everything to cheer them up. That matters so much to me; still does. Up until tonight, I felt a burden to everyone. My parents, friends, teachers, school mates, humanity basically. That's why I grew away from God. I blamed Him because that was the easy thing to do. Blame God for all your problems. He created you so He's responsible for your crappy life. Of course, now at this moment, I was blinded with spiritual pain. I was crushed by stress and pressure to be different, such as my grades, and helping my friends. My Spirit was beginning to get crushed. I was so incoherent to the fact that HE WAS THERE! He had my beautiful family

and friends there for me too. Being the stubborn girl I am, I chose to ignore that. I thought I could get over it; I was unaware to the fact that they were all there. They wanted to help, they cared! This was in seventh grade when I decided to be an inconsiderate idiot and make myself a social media account. That's what the "cool" people did. That made things worse. I as a person cannot handle something like that. I admit it now. For those who have never had an account, it sucks (excuse my language).

Chapter 2

Like a Rose

People judge you on how you pose for pictures, how you type, how many likes you get, the number of friends you have, your music, and cover picture. EVERYTHING. Needless to say at the time, I was trying to befriend a boy in my class and I posted a picture of a cut arm saying stop self harm, please share. His mom saw it and thought it was me and called my principal and youth director at church. I was called into the office and had a meeting with them. When I got home from school that day, I found my mom and dad sitting and I snottily said, "What did I do wrong?" My mom asked me to sit down and said we need to talk I immediately said, "I didn't make another account." She said it's not about that; please show us your arm. I started panicking and got a little lightheaded and barely got out "why?" She asked again and I started sobbing and showed them my hideous arm. I was humiliated, hurt, angry, and completely out of fight. The look on both of my parents' faces gave me complete shock and I was so amazed in a sickening way. The look on their faces was crushed disappointment as if they thought it was their fault.

The rest of the year, I blocked out everything with sadness. It worked for a while, but, the thing about self-harm is that it is addictive. Most people don't know, but, cutting or burning might as well be a drug because once you do it for a while, it's addicting. I didn't see glass or sharp objects as scary or dangerous. I thought of them as helpers. They were there when I couldn't confide about my cutting to anyone else. No one gets it. After a while, I was numb, nothing really felt anymore. I did it because I wanted to feel SOMETHING. To those who read this, I want you to know how hard I'm trying to explain this clearly. I liked cutting, it was a normal thing I did. It was a weekly thing, the consequences are the reminders, and I have 108 scars from self harm. I am actually ashamed of them. It's something I got through and survived. I have my spirit and attitude. I have my family and my music. The songs I listen to have so much emotion and beauty in a rough way. Like a rose, its beauty is protected by thorns. That's me, minus the beauty. I protect myself with cutting remarks and I don't trust most people.

Chapter 4

Acceptance, Faith, Visitors

This has been hard writing. I feel like I'm ruining myself by this, but, He is with me giving me strength. I have finally realized that all of my flaws—ADHD, anger issues, impulsiveness, and my weird emotions—make me who I am. I am fulfilled right now. I swear I have never felt so happy. I have realized a huge weight taken off my back. Stress dropped away. I was sitting here thinking how proud I am for trying so hard to make my parents proud, help my friends and make good decisions. Then I felt a presence; two actually.

I recognized one. I swear it was my aunt and she was urging me on and to keep going. I felt her aura. Mom and Dad you may not believe me, but, I felt someone else. He seemed happy and smart. I have no idea who it was, but, he said, "I am proud." I didn't see these people, I felt them laying here thinking and then it happened. You know how I said at the beginning of all this how I was skeptical of the Lord our God? Well, in one second, it changed. I know it was His work.

His power and confidence washing over me, refiguring me. I have Him on my side. I cried. I don't even know why I just felt so complete as if someone had taken a piece of my soul and then it was replaced tonight. I had to write it down. This is special; I know it is not fake. This is real I know it is because I have never felt this way before. I have never accepted God or the Christian faith until tonight. I never understood the commitment to be loyal and faithful to God, but now I do.

Chapter 5

I Have Plans, To Mom and Dad

It's huge and He's relying on us, His sons and daughters to help others and it feels so perfect. I feel so ashamed of not realizing the importance and beauty of faith. Mom and Dad, when you read this, I want to say thank you. I would not have been here without your support, love and commitment to give me the life and people I know. I know God has a plan for me I know that and I am working on trying to figure that out. I know I can sing and write, but, what good can that do for others? I have no idea but I will find out.

I did feel the reassurance of God and the most fulfilling feeling I have ever experienced. I am writing this specifically to my parents. I NEED them to know this because I want to do something drastic and maybe a bit crazy. I know my senior project is far away, but, I was thinking of going to middle schools around the city and talking about bullying, stress and the awfulness of cutting or burning and how people can help. I got out of that abyss didn't I? And I myself am extremely proud of me! I am positive that was not the end of my story. There are still many chapters, hundreds even. I plan on working hard. I did accept Him today and I chose to be a Christian and share my gifts and talents to God and people who need help or inspiration. I may be only 14, but I have plans bigger than I thought because of one night and one thought and one amazing family.

Chapter 6

Stand Still

I want to be remembered as a Christian singer or writer. I want to save people and mold the lives of younger ones that come after me. I want to preserve and help everyone's dreams the way I was given a chance after everything I've done.

If I end up getting medicine, it should help and make me a better student.

This has gotten so much off my chest and I thank God and Jesus. My life is in God's Hands. What He wants me to do, I will do.

"The Lord will fight for you all you need to do is stand still." —Exodus 14:14

This verse is my life verse. I follow it to trust God.

Like I said earlier, I was skeptical of God until I had that feeling tonight. It

was like, "Good job, see I've been watching you. You're safe and sound." This verse I found while wandering through the Bible on one of my sad days. I showed my mom and we both highlighted it. When I get confirmed, that's going to be my favorite verse because it applies to me. The Lord gave me strength to get through my sadness and self harm. He made sure I had people to help me. I was fighting against myself and He helped me by giving me a supportive family.

Chapter 7

Tehya's Poem

When you have courage and loved ones to pick you up
when you fall down, you can never fail.

Tehya's Poem

For He may watch over you

Silent guardian giver of life

Leader of love, protector of children

Teacher of forgiveness

Father of Christians and love.

The Lord is on my side, nothing can hurt me now.

The Lord will fight for you, you need only to be still

Exodus 14:14

Epilogue

I would like my daughter remembered as she stated in her journal as a good Christian girl who loved to sing and help others. The last year and a half of her life, the mental demons got her and she was lost.

I found this journal months after her death. I often wonder why she wrote this for us. As I think back to that happy smiling girl who loved to sing and help others, I realized that there was another side to her. I believe this journal explains all her deep feelings and why she did self-harm. She truly wanted to share these thoughts to help others not hurt as she did. She also wanted us to know that she appreciated us and the support and help we gave to her.

I know she is with God, safe and whole. We shall see her again.

Please, to those reading this book, if you don't feel safe, are scared, lonely, or suicidal, get help. Tell someone—parents, clergy, friends, or call the National Helpline at 1-800662-HELP (4357).

I close with Tehya's favorite Bible verse:

"The Lord will fight for you; you need only to be still." —Exodus 14

Norma Lundstrom

Norma Lundstrom is a retired teacher
living in Kenosha, Wisconsin
with her husband and their dog, Max.

Other books by Norma include:
The Chubby Girl
All Families are Special
Dogs, Ducks & Devotion
Jars of Clay

You can find her books on Amazon.com.
If you enjoy this book or any of her other books,

please post a review on Amazon.

Thank you!

putty in their hands and they made me who I am. They taught me to be polite, nice, stand tall and don't let anyone tell you you're not worth it. I believe I am generally a good Christian person.

I am not the best with school. I am terrible at spelling. Sometimes letters jumble together in my head. One of my teachers told me my mind works faster than my pen. I'm always getting new ideas and forgetting them. That's why it's helpful to write every thought down.

Also math and numbers mash together and make no sense. I try so hard to focus and then I get a headache. I found listening to music when I do homework helps me.

I have trouble focusing and controlling my anger. I have random emotions. Sometimes I can't really control it. One day I really don't feel like talking and another I'm super hyper and happy. This is the part where I connect The Father, God, and Lord. These are my raw, exposed feelings.

Chapter 3

Different Than Most, Special

I need to know the person to trust then. That doesn't happen often due to the fact of me not opening up. I have a shield from everything, a mental block to protect me from everything. That's how I got through 5th, 6th, and 7th grade.

I was bullied for years. I never told anyone until 5th grade. Everyone was saying terrible things about me. I was naïve and was thinking why me? But then, I faced reality and realized it's because I'm different than most. I used to be quirky and flighty and went place to place and never sat still. I blurted things out and didn't think the effect the words had on others. I didn't care what others thought. I thought I was normal and then found out I was adopted. I thought, "Oh that's awesome, I'm special." I found out who my birth mom was and was crushed. My grandparents adopted me and I tried hard not to be like her, their daughter. I started worrying about everything I did to be opposite of her. I got led off track basically by choices I made. I'm not perfect, but, I was raised by amazing people. They shaped me into who I am right now. I was

The Lord will
fight for you,
you need only
to be still.

Exodus 14:14

Made in the USA
Monee, IL
15 September 2022